Countries of the World: A Primary Source Journey

A Primary Source Guide to

CHILE

Christopher Blomquist

The Rosen Publishing Group's

PowerKids Press™
PRIMARY SOURCE

New York

For Lisa D., con amor

Published in 2005 by The Rosen Publishing Group, Inc.
29 East 21st Street, New York, NY 10010

First Edition

Editor: Kathy Kuhtz Campbell
Book Design: Haley Wilson
Layout Design: Michael J. Caroleo
Photo Researcher: Adriana Skura

Photo Credits: Cover, p. 6 © Michael Andrews/Earth Scenes; p. 4 © 2002 Geo Atlas; p. 6 (inset) © Stefano Nicolini/Earth Scenes; p. 8 © Charles & Josette Lenars/Corbis, (inset) © Archivo Nacional Historico; p. 10 © Charles O'Rear/Corbis, (inset) © AP/Wide World Photos; p. 12 © Hubertus Kanus/Photo Researchers, Inc, (inset) © Linda Phillips/Photo Researchers, Inc; p. 14 © David Frazier/The Image Works; p. 16 © South American Pictures; p. 18 Jorge Ianiszewski/Art Resource, NY; p. 19 © Hulton/Archive/Getty Images; p. 20 © Barnabas Bosshart/Corbis, (inset) Paul Jenkin/Earth Scenes.

Library of Congress Cataloging-in-Publication Data

Blomquist, Christopher.
A primary source guide to Chile / Christopher Blomquist.— 1st ed.
   p. cm. — (Countries of the world, a primary source journey)
Summary: Introduces the geography, history, culture, and traditions of the South American nation, Chile.
Includes bibliographical references and index.
ISBN 1-4042-2751-2 (Library Binding)
1. Chile—Juvenile literature. [1. Chile.] I. Title. II. Series.
F3058.5 .B56 2005
983—dc22
                      2003017817

Manufactured in the United States of America

Contents

PERU

Pacific
Ocean

BOLIVIA

BRAZIL

PARAGUAY

El Tatio Geysers

Asunción

Atacama Desert

CHILE

ANDES

Easter Island

URUGUAY

ARGENTINA

Montevideo

Santiago

Buenos Aires

Juan Fernández
Islands

Atlantic
Ocean

ANDES

Strait of Magellan

Tierra Del
Fuego

4

South America's String Bean

Chile is a long, narrow country that runs along the western edge of South America. It is shaped somewhat like a string bean. Chile has an area of 292,133 square miles (756,621 sq km). The countries Peru, Bolivia, and Argentina border Chile. The Andes mountain range runs along Chile's eastern border from northern Chile all the way to its southern tip. Chile also owns some small islands far out west in the Pacific Ocean. These are the Juan Fernández islands and Easter Island.

More than 15 million people live in Chile. One-third of the total population lives in or near Santiago, Chile's capital.

◄ Chile's coastline, which runs along the Pacific Ocean, is 3,999 miles (6,435 km) long. At Chile's southern tip are the islands that make up Tierra del Fuego, or "land of fire."

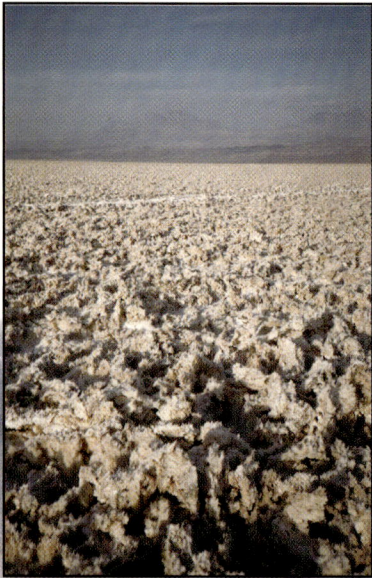

Deserts, Rich Valleys, and Glaciers

The Atacama Desert makes up Chile's Norte Grande, or "great north" area. In the Atacama Desert, El Tatio **geysers**, the world's tallest, let out steam high into the air early every morning. Just south of Norte Grande is Norte Chico, or the "little north" region. This area is dry but it has some forests. Central Chile has wet winters and dry summers. Below central Chile is Sur Chico, or "little south." This rainy, mild area is also called the lake country. It is forest-covered land. Chile's southernmost regions, Patagonia and Tierra del Fuego, are rainy and cold. Patagonia and Tierra del Fuego are windy and wild places. These areas include plains called pampas, rocky islands, volcanoes, and **glaciers**.

The geysers of El Tatio in Chile's Central Valley shoot jets of water as high as 20 feet (6 m) into the air. *Inset*: Many scientists believe that in some places of the Atacama Desert, rain has not fallen in more than 400 years.

8

Chile's Past

People were living in Chile more than 13,000 years ago. By A.D. 1400, some Native American peoples, such as the Mapuche, Aymara, and Inca, had villages in Chile. In fact, the name Chile comes from the Native American word *tchili*, which means "snow."

In 1541, Spaniard Pedro de Valdivia claimed Chile as a Spanish **colony** and set up Santiago and other towns. On September 18, 1810, nationalists won a fight to break away from the Spanish governor who still ruled Chile. Chilean Bernardo O'Higgins helped to beat Spanish troops in 1817. **Independence** became official in 1818. Today September 18 is observed as Chile's Independence Day.

This rock carving shows a figure called the Birdman that was cut into the cliffs of Orongo on Easter Island. The Birdman, half man and half bird, was honored in the native religion from the 1680s to the 1860s. *Inset*: This document, signed by Pedro de Valdivia in 1541, established Chile as a Spanish colony.

The Republic of Chile

The **Republic** of Chile in the 1800s was much smaller than it is today. Starting in 1879, Chile fought a war against Bolivia over ownership of copper mines. Chile won the war and grew to its present-day size by taking lands from Bolivia.

Chile was a **democratic** government until 1973. That year, a **dictator**, General Augusto Pinochet Ugarte, took over. He took away many freedoms. In the 1980s, huge numbers of Chileans pressed Pinochet to hold an election. In 1989, they voted not to give him another term as president. Instead they chose Patricio Aylwin, who became president in March 1990. Today Chile is democratic again.

The Chuquicamata Copper Mine in Codelco, Chile, is one of the world's largest. *Inset*: Ricardo Lagos was elected president of Chile in 2000. The people elect the president every six years.

The Chilean Economy

Mining in regions such as Norte Grande is an important part of the Chilean economy. Copper accounts for about 40 percent of the goods that Chile exports, or sends to other countries, each year.

Chile also earns money from **industries** such as forestry, fishing, farming, winemaking, and travel. Of the 5.9 million workers in Chile, many work in service and government jobs, in manufacturing and trade, or on farms, in fishing, or in forestry. Some Chileans work in construction and mining. About 22 percent of Chileans are poor and 7 percent of Chile's citizens do not have jobs.

Raising sheep is an important industry, especially in southern Chile. *Inset:* A worker in an alpaca mill checks the wool as it comes off a machine. An alpaca is an animal in the camel family. *Above:* Chile's money is the pesos. This 2000 pesos note shows the Chilean hero Manuel Rodríguez Erdoyza.

Different Peoples and Two Last Names

Eight out of ten people who live in Chile have both Native American ancestors, or relatives who lived long ago, and European ancestors. These people of mixed ancestry are called mestizos. About one million pure-blooded Native American Mapuche people also live in Chile. Spanish is the official language of Chile. Some Chileans, such as the Mapuche, also speak a Native American language known as Mapudungun.

Most Chileans use their father's last name and their mother's last name after their given first name. Though many Chileans have a two-part surname, or last name, people tend to use only the first part. For example, teacher Rosa Ruiz Allende is called Ms. Ruiz.

A Mapuche woman plays the *kultrún*, a kind of drum. The name Mapuche is made up of two words, *mapu*, which means "earth" or "land," and *che*, which means "people." Many Mapuche live in the southern city of Temuco. This city is in an area called Los Lagos, also known as the lake country.

Nearly 90 percent of Chile's population is **Catholic**. Catholicism was the official religion of Chile until 1925. In that year, the Chilean government did away with the idea of having a national religion. People can practice any religion they wish. The other 10 percent of Chile's population includes mostly **Protestants**.

From July 12 to July 18 each year the people of La Tirana, a town in Norte Grande, pay respect to the Virgin of Carmen. They dance and parade in the streets in colorful costumes. Chileans also honor their Independence Day, September 18, by attending parades, gathering for fun in local parks, flying kites, and doing the *cueca*, Chile's national dance.

Chile's Independence Day is honored on September 18 each year. Everyone dances the *cueca*, the country's national dance. Partners dance around each other without touching and wave handkerchiefs.

18

The Arts

Chile has artists of all kinds. Its cultural centers allow Chileans to enjoy drama, ballet, classical music, and paintings. Two such centers are the Municipal Theater and the Fine Arts Museum, which are both located in Santiago.

Two Chilean poets, Gabriela Mistral and Pablo Neruda, are well known because they both won the **Nobel Prize**. Mistral won her Nobel Prize in 1945 for her five collections of poetry. Neruda won his Nobel Prize in 1971 for collections such as *Canto general*, which was printed in 1950 and includes Neruda's famous poem "The Heights of Macchu Picchu."

This Mapuche weaving shows the kinds of images and patterns that were often used instead of writing in the Mapuche culture. *Above*: Pablo Neruda, who lived from 1904 to 1973, is one of Chile's most widely read poets.

Chile Today

Although Chile has a bright future overall, its government still has several problems to solve. A 2001 report claimed that Santiago has the second-most-polluted air in the Americas after Mexico City, Mexico. Conama, the Chilean government's **environmental** agency, is working to solve the pollution problems and to protect Chile's lands and natural treasures.

Chile is attracting more travelers. In 2000 alone, 1,742,666 people visited Chile. They hiked in the country's national parks, shopped and explored in Chile's cities, and tasted local dishes. Chile's sights and charm delighted them!

The capital city, Santiago, is located near the Andes. Because of the city's location between the Andes and nearby hills, Santiago gets very little wind. Air pollution from automobiles is a major problem. *Inset:* Grey Glacier, a popular sight for visitors, is located in Torres del Paine National Park in southern Chile.

Chile at a Glance

Population: 15,498,930

Capital City: Santiago, population about 5,500,000

Largest City: Santiago

Official Name: Republic of Chile

National Anthem: "Himno Nacional de Chile" ("National Anthem of Chile")

Land Area: 292,133 square miles (756,621 sq km)

Government: Republic

Unit of Money: Peso

Flag: Chile's flag has red and white **horizontal** stripes and a blue square with a white star. The white stripe stands for the snow of the Andes, the red stripe is for the blood of the loyal Chileans, and the blue square is for the sky. The star stands for the national government.

Glossary

Catholic (KATH-lik) Belonging to the Roman Catholic faith.

colony (KAH-luh-nee) A new land that is claimed for the government of another country.

democratic (deh-muh-KRA-tik) In favor of democracy, a system in which people choose their leaders.

dictator (DIK-tay-ter) A person who takes power and has total control over others.

environmental (en-vy-ern-MEN-tel) Relating to all the living things and conditions of a place.

geysers (GY-zerz) Explosions of hot water and steam from a crack in Earth's surface.

glaciers (GLAY-shurz) Large masses of ice that move down a mountain or along a valley.

horizontal (hor-ih-ZON-til) Going from side to side.

independence (in-dih-PEN-dents) Freedom or self-rule.

industries (IN-dus-treez) Businesses in which many people work and make money producing a product.

Nobel Prize (noh-BEL PRYZ) An award of money given each year to a person or a group for working in a subject, such as writing.

Protestants (PRAH-tes-tunts) People who belong to a Christian-based church but who are not Catholic.

republic (ree-PUB-lik) A form of government in which the authority belongs to the people.

23

Index

Primary Source List

Page 6. El Tatio geysers are located near San Pedro de Atacama. The geyser field is located in a valley in the mountains of the Andes and is surrounded by active volcanoes. The geysers, which number more than 100, are the highest in the world, and they were formed as a result of water boiling through the porous volcanic rock.

Page 8. Petroglyphs stand on Easter Island, Chile. It is not known when these rock carvings were made or who made them, but it is believed that they might date from the second century. The rock carvings are located in many areas of the island, and the best examples can be seen on smooth areas of volcanic rocks. One of the most popular images on Easter Island is the birdman image, which is connected to a native cult.

Page 8 (inset). This document established Santiago as a Spanish settlement and capital of Chile. Pedro de Valdivia signed it on February 2, 1541.

Page 18. This Mapuche weaving is located in the Museum of Pre-Columbian Art in Santiago, Chile.

Page 19. Pablo Neruda was born Neftalí Ricardo Reyes y Basoalto. He began writing poetry under the name Pablo Neruda at the age of 16. Chile's best-known poet, Neruda was photographed here on January 18, 1952.

Web Sites

Due to the changing nature of Internet links, PowerKids Press has developed an online list of Web sites related to the subject of this book. This site is updated regularly. Please use this link to access the list:
www.powerkidslinks.com/cwpsj/pschil/